20th Century
INVENTIONS

Jenna Winterberg

Publishing Credits

Rachelle Cracchiolo, M.S.Ed., *Publisher*
Conni Medina, M.A.Ed., *Managing Editor*
Nika Fabienke, Ed.D., *Series Developer*
June Kikuchi, *Content Director*
John Leach, *Assistant Editor*
Kevin Pham, *Graphic Designer*

TIME For Kids and the TIME For Kids logo are registered trademarks of TIME Inc. Used under license.

Image Credits: pp.4–5, 11 Granger, NYC; p.5 (inset) Vintage Images/Alamy Stock Photo; p.6 (bottom) Bettmann/Getty Images; p.9 Library of Congress [LC-DIG-ggbain-30251]; p.13 Illustration by Timothy J. Bradley; p.17 (ENIAC computer) Pictorial Press Ltd/Alamy Stock Photo, (Compaq Plus) INTERFOTO/Alamy Stock Photo; p.24 (bottom) Getty Images; all other images from iStock and/or Shutterstock.

All companies and products mentioned in this book are registered trademarks of their respective owners or developers and are used in this book strictly for editorial purposes; no commercial claim to their use is made by the author or the publisher.

Teacher Created Materials

5301 Oceanus Drive
Huntington Beach, CA 92649-1030
http://www.tcmpub.com
ISBN 978-1-4258-4971-9
© 2018 Teacher Created Materials, Inc.

Table of Contents

Table of Contents 3

The Past Is Present 4

A Dream Home 6

Streets to Space 13

High-Tech Life 16

Back to the Future 27

Glossary 28

Index 29

Check It Out! 30

Try It! 31

The Past Is Present

The year is 1900. Only a few homes have **electric** wiring and running water. People travel by foot, horse, or even **streetcar**. The world is changing.

Inventors of the time want to make the pace of life faster and easier. But what will people do with their free time? Brilliant minds will work to come up with many new things. Soon, there will be a world of options.

20th Century U.S. Transportation

Amount of	1900	1999
horses	22 million	5 million
train tracks	193,000 miles	144,500 miles
streetcar tracks	16,645 miles	191 miles
cars	8,000	208 million
paved roads	144	4 million

horse-drawn carriage in the early 20th century

A Dream Home

Modern homes would seem like a fantasy to a person from the early 20th century. We use many amazing devices today! We watch TVs. We email and shop using computers. Machines wash our dishes and clothes.

Cooking is not the chore it used to be. Making bread used to take eight hours. Now, we have sliced bread and toasters. We buy premade foods. We heat meals in microwave ovens.

Early microwaves were huge! This one is from the 1950s.

Time line of Household Inventions

- 1900
- **1902** — air conditioner, flashlight
- **1903** — coat hanger
- **1907** — paper towels
- **1908** — domestic vacuum
- 1910
- **1911** — electric washing maching
- **1913** — refrigerator
- **1919** — toaster
- 1920
- **1920** — handheld hair dryer
- **1927** — shampoo
- **1928** — sliced bread
- **1929** — frozen food
- 1930
- **1938** — electric dryer, toothbrush

The Real Dirt

What inspires invention? For James Spangler, it was asthma. His job was to clean an entire department store each night. But his sweeping stirred up dust that bothered his lungs.

Spangler had an idea. He put an electric motor on his sweeper. Then, he added fan blades. The motor turned the blades to suck up dirt. All he needed was a place to collect the dirt. He used a pillowcase.

Spangler solved his problem. He invented the portable electric vacuum.

A woman uses a vacuum in the early 20th century.

Cool Kitchen

Kitchens have come a long way. Not all advances have to do with cooking. Keeping food cold helps it last longer. It also makes food safer to eat.

In the past, people used iceboxes. Food was kept cold in wooden boxes. These boxes had blocks of ice in them.

In 1913, Fred Wolf put an electric unit on top. Cold air kept the boxes cold. The refrigerator was born.

Inspired by a Candy Bar

Microwaves use light waves that we can't see. Percy Spencer worked at a **radar** test station. The candy bar in his pocket melted when he walked near the equipment. He realized that radar waves could heat food.

A boy loads ice into an icebox.

Streets to Space

Inventions have helped make it safe and easy to travel. Injuries from cars used to be common. The drivers were not the ones at risk. People on foot faced danger from cars on crowded streets. Traffic lights helped fix the problem.

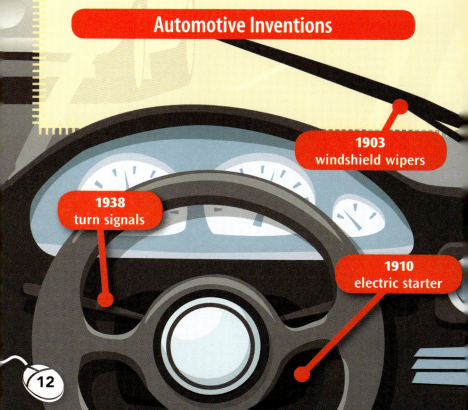

Automotive Inventions

1903 windshield wipers

1938 turn signals

1910 electric starter

Road trips became popular as the cost of owning a car came down. They became even more common when highways were built to link cities. People used to take trips on trains and ships. Soon, airplanes became more popular. Planes made travel faster.

Travel to outer space was not far behind. In 1969, the United States sent men to the moon and back!

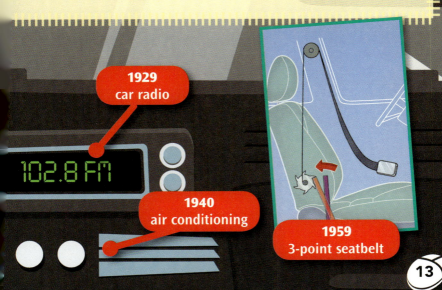

1929 car radio

1940 air conditioning

1959 3-point seatbelt

The Jet-Set Era

The Wright brothers took their first flight in 1903. Three decades later, the first airliner still had just 10 seats. For a long time, only the rich could afford to fly. World War II changed that.

The United States needed better fighter planes for the war. This led to three important inventions in the 1940s. First came cabin pressure. Planes could now fly higher. Next came jet **engines**. Planes could go farther and faster. Then came radar tools. Flights became safer.

After the war, air travel boomed. Jets became bigger. Many people now had the chance to fly.

Rocket Power

Jet engines gave rocket power a boost. That let new probes and **satellites** leave Earth. NASA used rockets to send men to the moon. NASA also built space shuttles for repeat trips.

High-Tech Life

For many people, it is hard to picture what life was like before computers. Computers were huge when they were first invented! One machine weighed 50 tons (45 metric tons). Huge tech gave way to high tech over time. Now, just one **microchip** in a laptop can do more than the first computers could.

People rely on technology. It helps them do things faster. It frees up time. Inventors try to improve tech all the time.

From Big to Small

1940

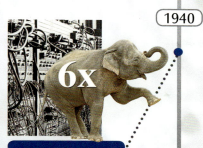

1946
The 1946 ENIAC computer weighed as much as 6 elephants.

1970

1975
The 1975 IBM portable computer weighed as much as a husky.

2000

1999
By 1999, some laptops weighed less than 3 pounds, about the weight of a 12-week-old kitten.

Music to Go

One hundred years ago, people listened to music on phonographs. These machines played cylinders with sound recorded on them. Vinyl records came after that. They could hold more songs. They had better sound, too.

But people wanted to listen to music in more places. Soon, 8-track tapes, cassette tapes, and compact discs (CDs) were created. People could listen to music in the car or on a walk. Each new invention was smaller and easier to store. And each offered better sound. Then, with the MP3, music went digital.

Modern Music Media

Format	Invented	Benefit
vinyl record	1948	long play time
cassette	1962	small size
8-track	1963	use on the road
CD	1982	high quality
MP3	1994	easy to store

Sing Along

In 1969, a musician in Japan had an idea. He could not always play music for his friend who liked singing. To solve this, he made the karaoke (kehr-ee-OH-kee) machine. It plays music you can sing along to!

Watch the Tube

Vacuum tubes gave life to TVs. The tubes were invented in 1904. They focus waves of light. This creates pictures on the screen. These tubes are in other machines, too. You can find them in radios and computers.

In the 1950s, TVs changed again. They became faster and smaller. Transistors changed the way electricity was used in TVs and other machines. This led to even faster and smaller devices.

In Color

The first TV sets that could show color were invented in the 1940s. But they were expensive, and many stations did not show programs in color. TVs became cheaper in the '60s, and more programs were made in color.

Building an Audience

Year	TVs in the United States
1945	10,000
1950	6 million
1960	60 million
1997	219 million

Call Me Anytime

The first cell phones were sold in 1983. People were excited about this new invention. But the first cell phone was huge! People wanted smaller phones. Over time, cell phones became smaller and sleeker. They went digital. Digital phones are like digital clocks. They have no moving parts. Digital tech takes up less space.

In recent years, people want more from their phones. They want to take pictures and play games with their phones. To make this possible, cell phones have become larger.

early handheld cell phone

Picture This

Simple emoticons show emotion using regular keys on a keyboard. The smiling face— :) —is one of the most common emoticons. Then, new symbols were created. They are called *emoji*. The smiling face became this: ☺. From faces to scenes, these symbols can send messages without words.

Medical Aid

In 1918, a lot of people died from the flu. Doctors worked to find out what caused diseases. So, they studied blood. They learned about **bacteria**. This led to vaccines, which save lives.

Doctors started to use new materials to help sick people. They learned that **titanium** could fuse with bones. They used it to fix broken bones. Plastic could be used inside the body, too. Doctors even made a mechanical heart!

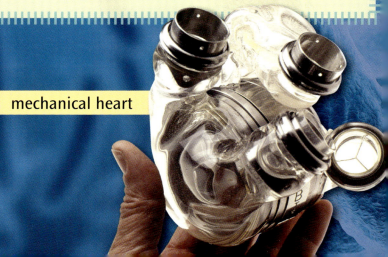

mechanical heart

20th Century Medical Inventions

- 1900
- **1907** blood-type testing
- 1910
- 1920
- **1920** Band-Aid
- 1930
- **1932** blood bank
- 1940
- **1943** mass production of penicillin
- **1950** blood bag
- 1950
- **1952** polio vaccine
- 1960
- **1963** measles vaccine
- **1967** mumps vaccine
- 1970
- **1971** soft contact lenses
- 1980
- **1982** artificial heart implant

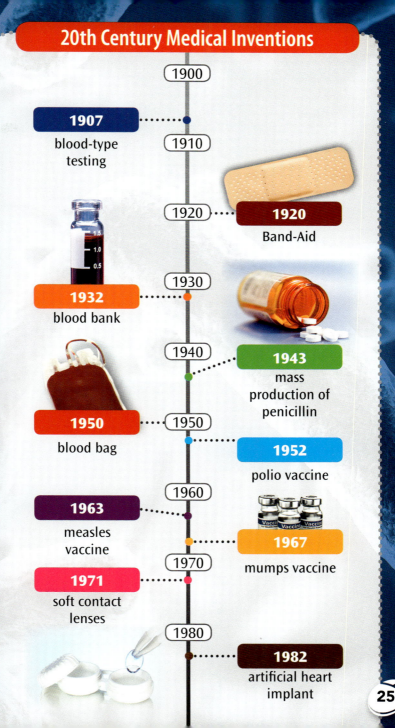

Back to the Future

Trying to invent something can be like solving a puzzle. The picture is hard to see before the pieces are in the right place. Some inventions take a long time to develop. Others are made quickly. Some things we have today seemed impossible one hundred years ago.

But people worked hard to make them real. Many new devices were created in the 20th century. People saw problems and tried to fix them. They wanted to make life easier. That is how cars, TVs, and microwave ovens came to be. Now, many people cannot live without these inventions!

Fly Me to the Mall

What hovers and can travel between towns like trains of old? A flying car, of course. One company has big plans to release the tech by 2021.

Glossary

bacteria—extremely small creatures that can be seen only through a microscope

electric—relating to electricity, a type of energy used in machines

engines—machines for driving or operating something

microchip—a small computer circuit

radar—a system to detect objects like planes and ships

satellites—objects that orbit any object in space to collect data

streetcar—a kind of public transportation that runs on rails

titanium—a strong, light metal that naturally fuses with human bone

Index

airplane, 13

car, 5, 12–13, 18, 27

CD, 18–19

cell phone, 22–23

computer, 6, 16–17, 20

email, 6, 16

Internet, 16, 23

jet, 14–15

karaoke, 19

microchip, 16

microwave, 6, 11

MP3, 18–19

radio, 13, 18, 20

refrigerator, 7, 10

satellite, 15

space shuttle, 15

Spangler, James, 8

TV, 6, 20–21, 27

train, 5, 13, 27

vaccine, 24–25

vacuum, 7–9

vacuum tube, 20

Wolf, Fred, 10

Wright brothers, 14

Check It Out!

Books

Tesar, Jenny, and Bryan Bunch. 2001. *The Blackbirch Encyclopedia of Science & Invention*. Blackbirch Press, Inc.

Editors of TIME FOR KIDS Magazine. 2015. *Book of WHAT: Everything Inventions*. TIME FOR KIDS.

Videos

David Harris Katz Entertainment, Inc. *Wow, I Never Knew That!* David Harris Katz Entertainment, Inc.

Nash, Bruce. *Modern Marvels*. The History Channel.

Websites

Smithsonian National Air and Space Museum. *Engineering the Wright Way*. airandspace.si.edu/.

Various. *Who Made That?* www.nytimes.com/column/magazine-innovation.

Try It!

What is your favorite invention that is explained in this book?

- What do you like about it? What do you not like?
- How could you make the invention better?
- Write a paragraph about your ideas. Or draw a picture and label the parts of your invention.
- Share your idea with your class.

About the Author

Jenna Winterberg started writing for print publications when she was in high school. She has worked on catalogs, magazines, and books. She loves science, the outdoors, and travel. She lives in Los Angeles, where she puts science to use as a personal trainer.

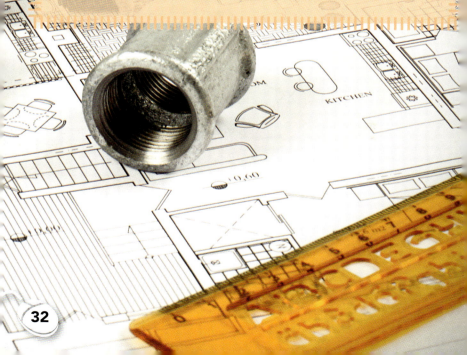